AF338290

Dreaming Along the Laurel

Jason Bruner
Keeley Bruner

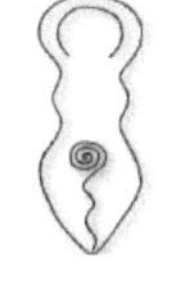

Thea Press

Dreaming Along the Laurel

by Jason Bruner and Keeley Bruner

Thea Press
P.O. Box 24905
Tempe, AZ 85285
www.theapress.org

ISBN-13: 978-1-956604-02-3 (Hardcover)

To Julia, Kathryn, and Joel

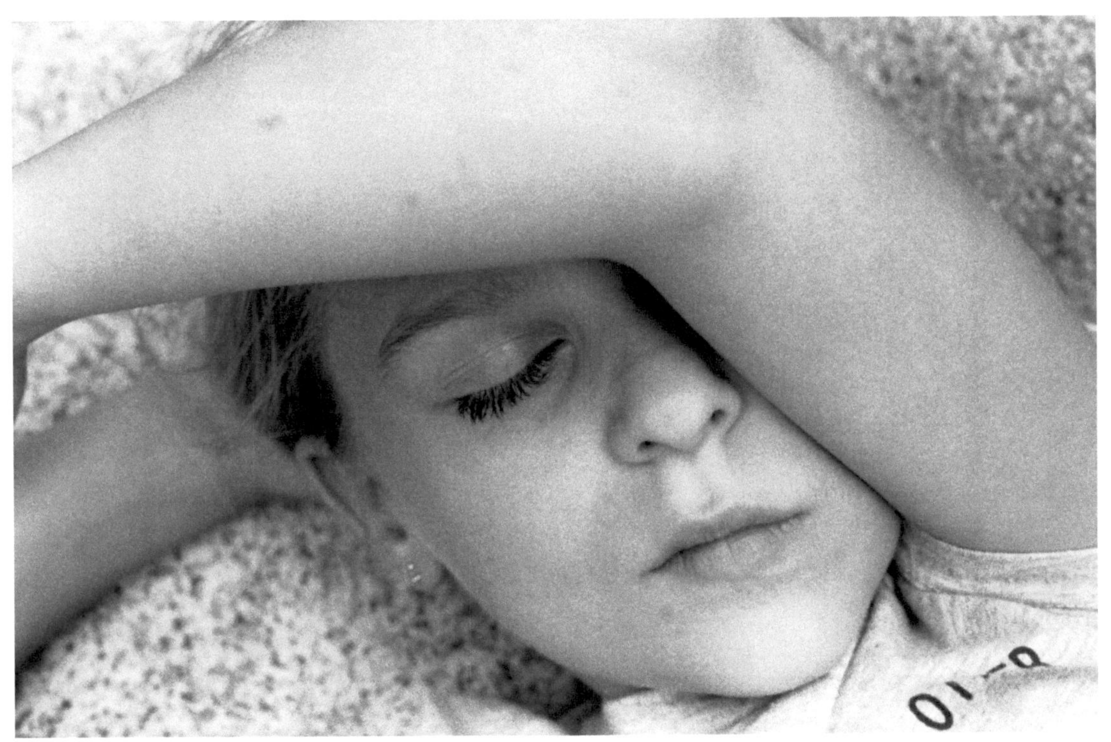

It's not really like talking.

It's more like a feeling of words.

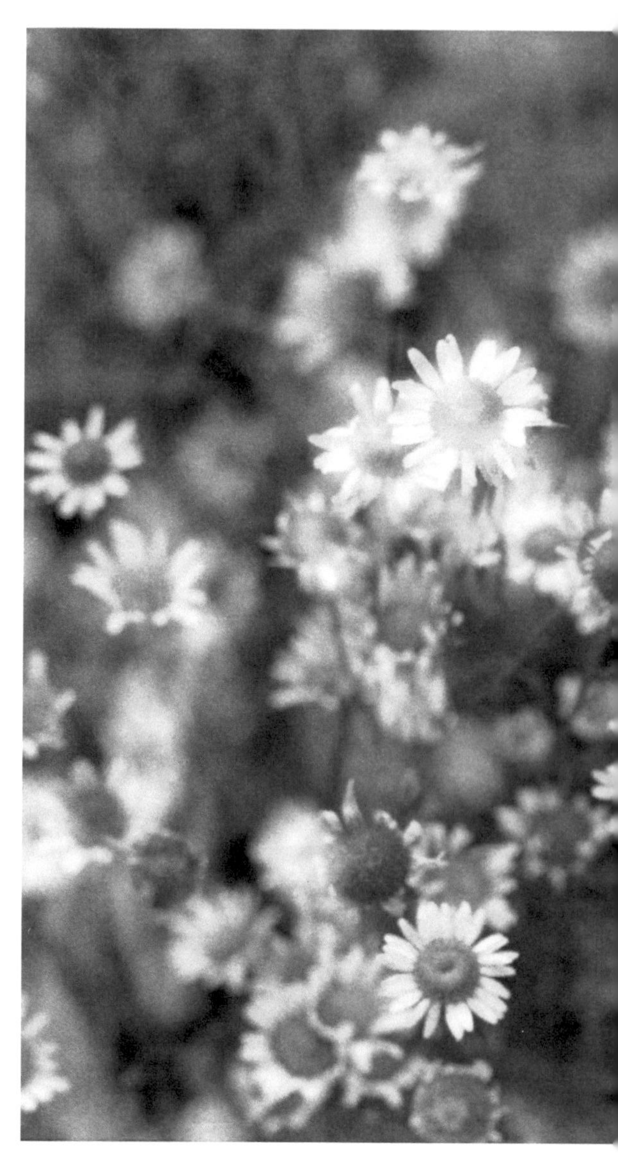

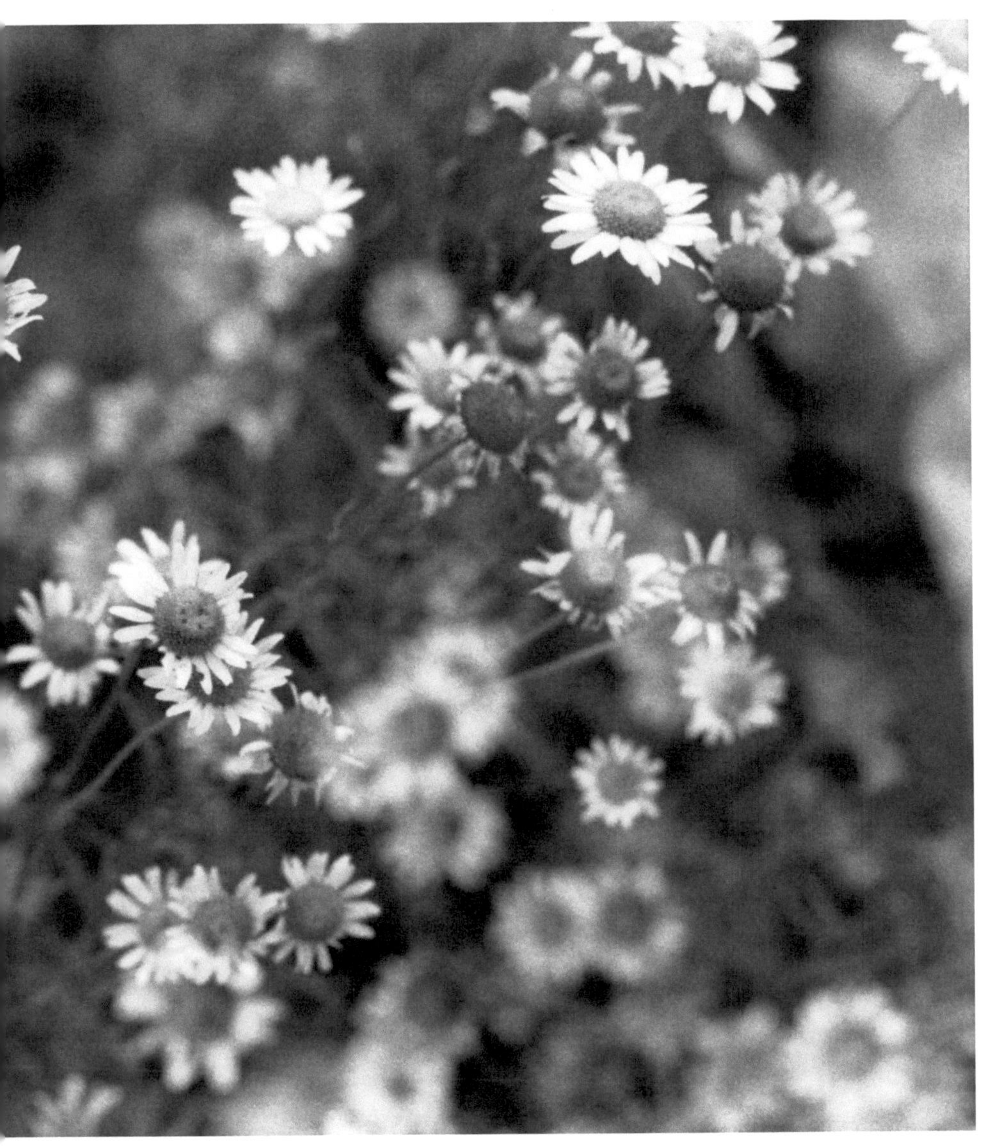

Drowsy chimes twinkle, thin like God speaking in the wind,

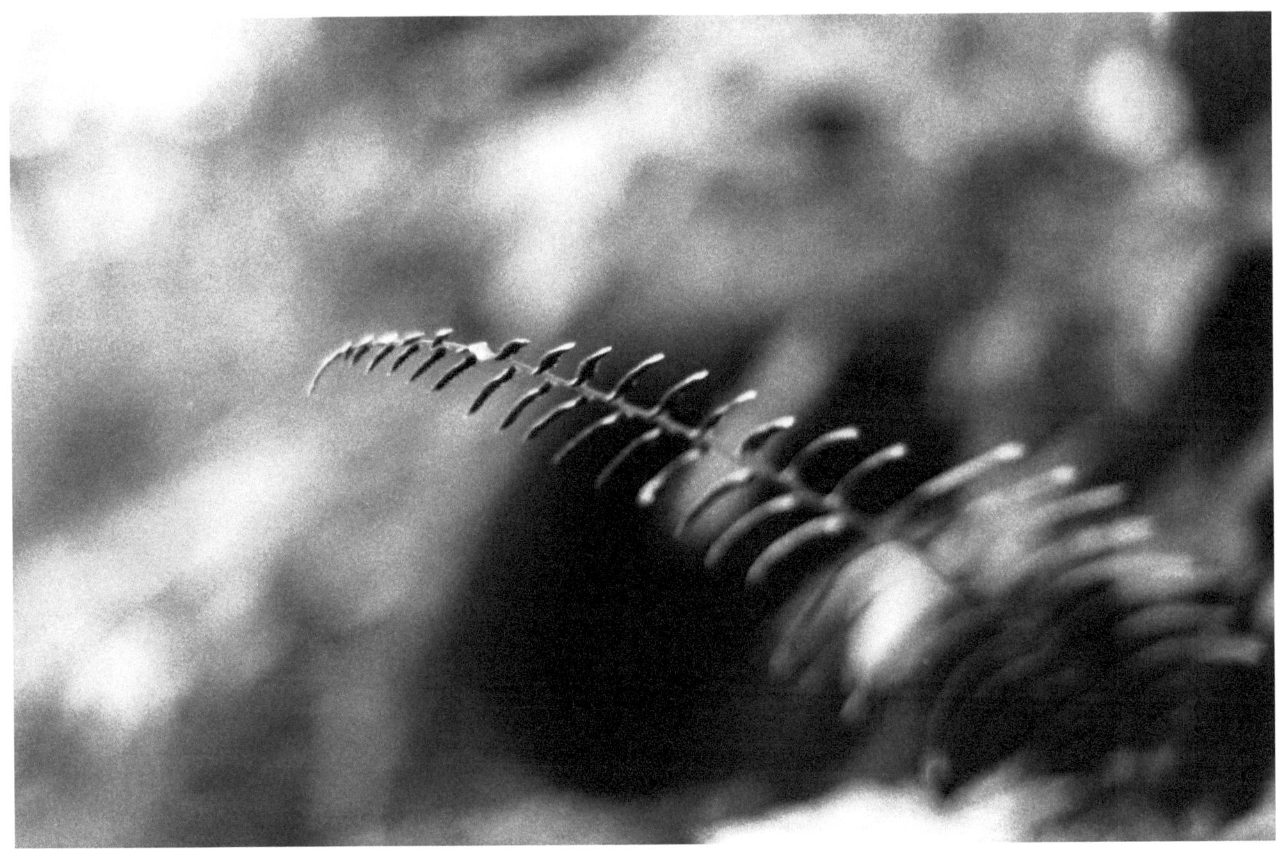

but the dark is still and music is not song.

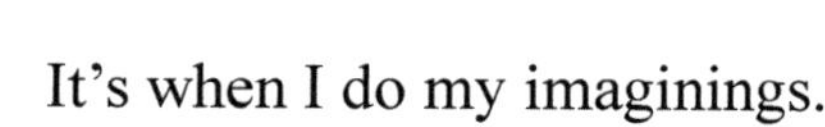

It's when I do my imaginings.

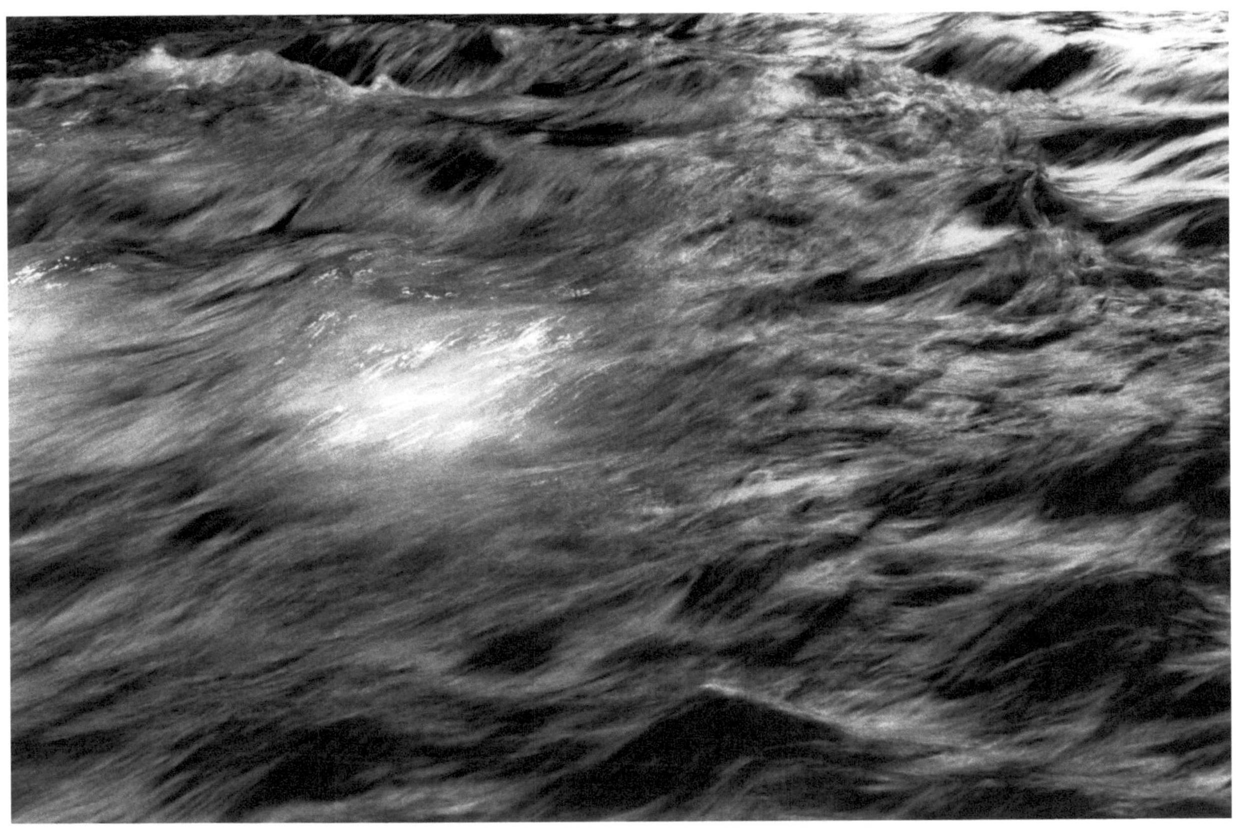

Sleep is rhythm she makes but cannot hear.

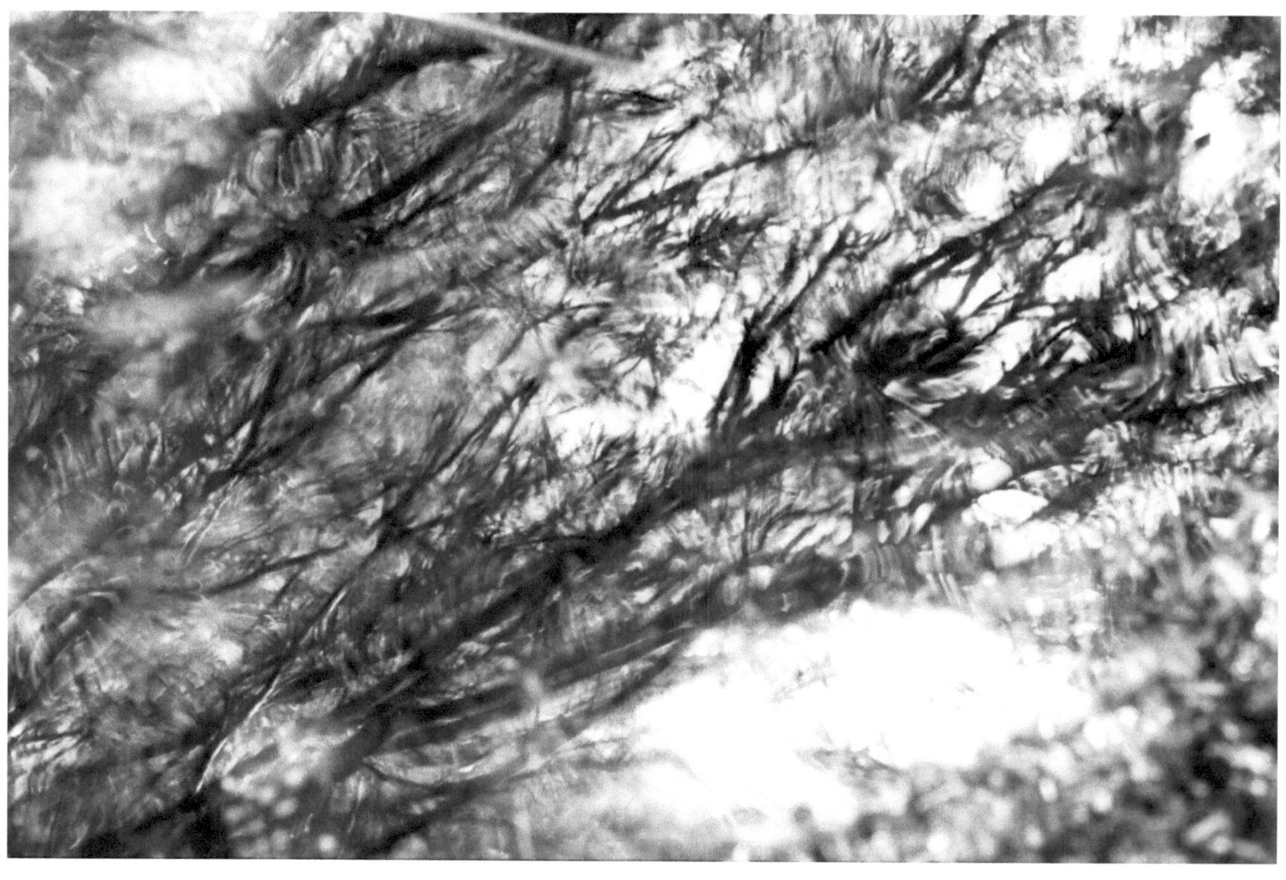

At dawn, she tells me our daughter cried out in the night.

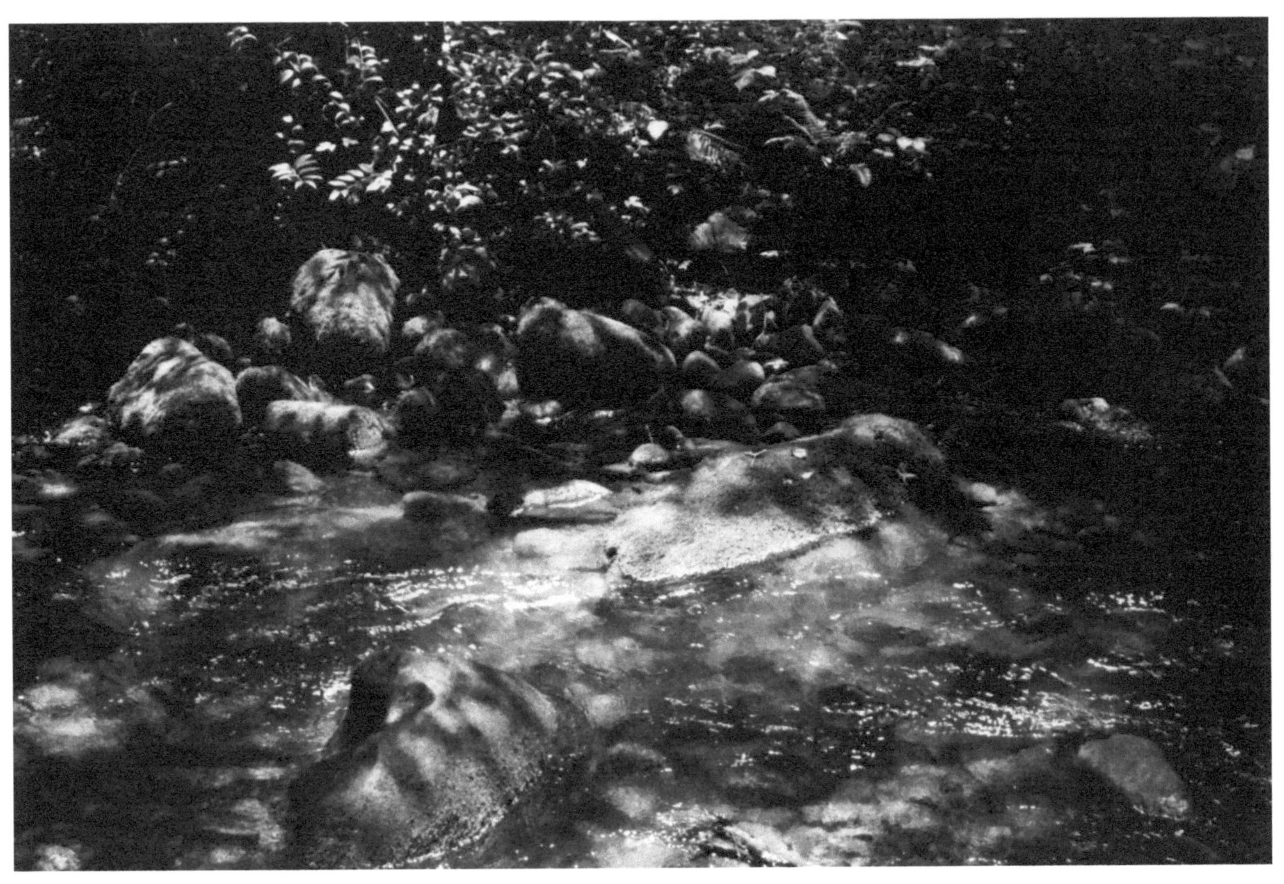

I felt I was losing my memories.

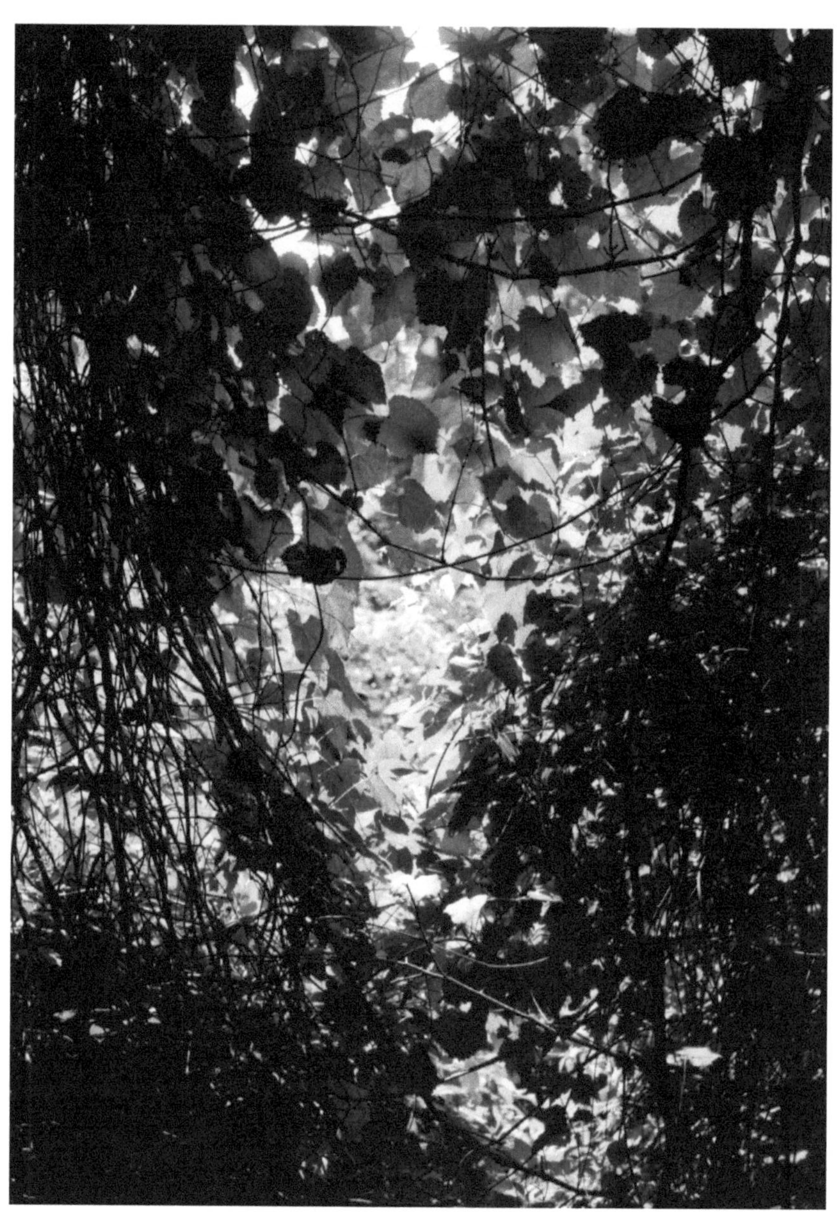

Otherwise, I would not have known.

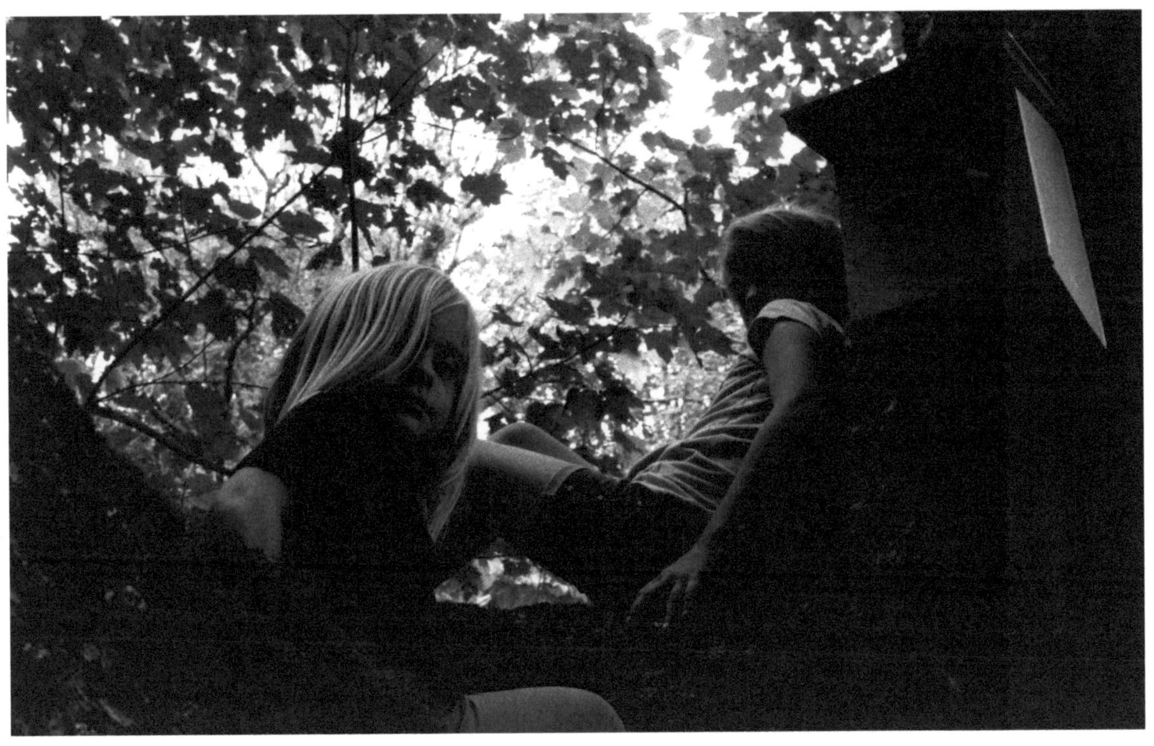

You are a good memory-er! she tells her sister.

But it's hard to hold on to what you know,

when everything can be something else also.

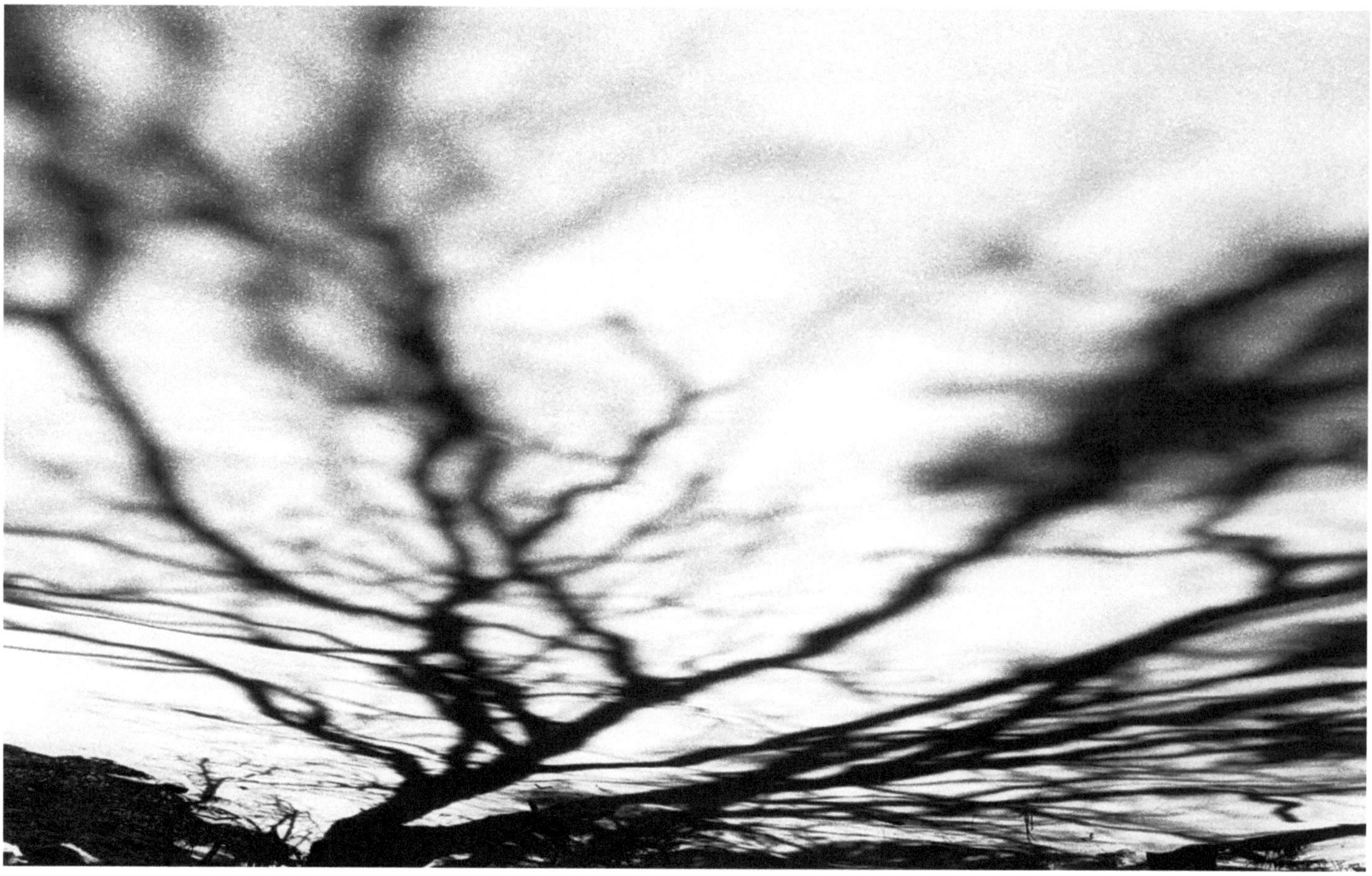

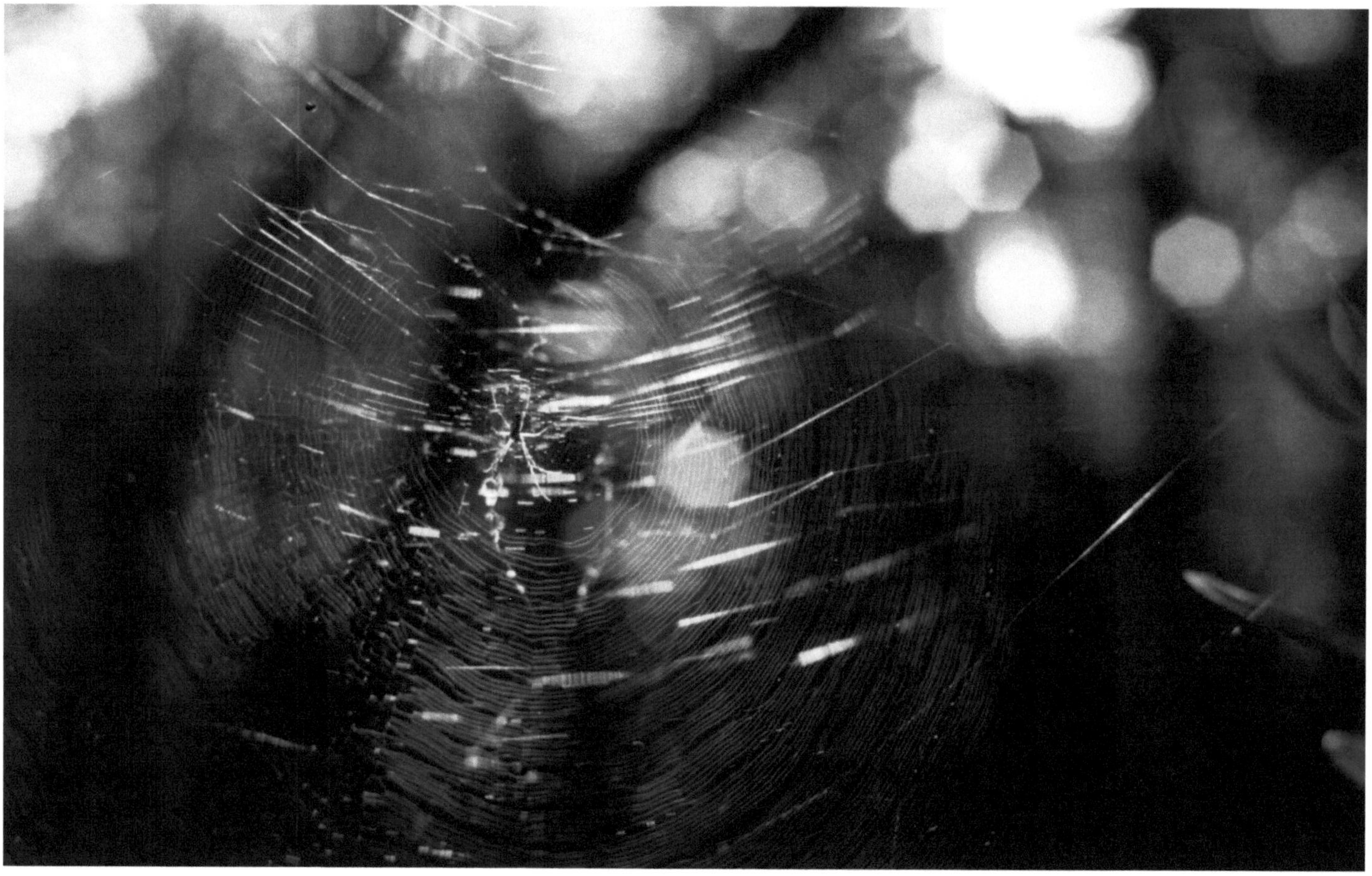

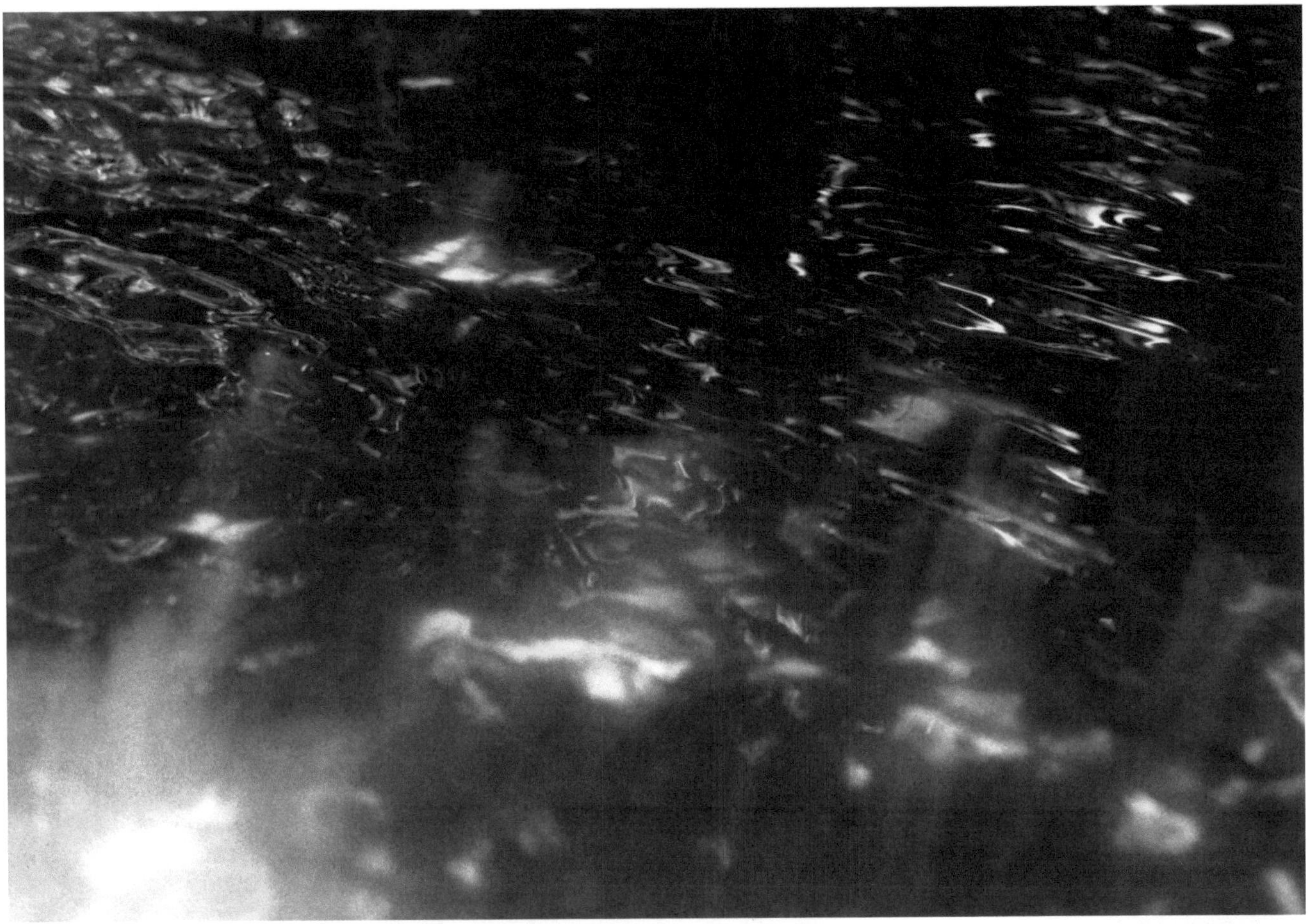

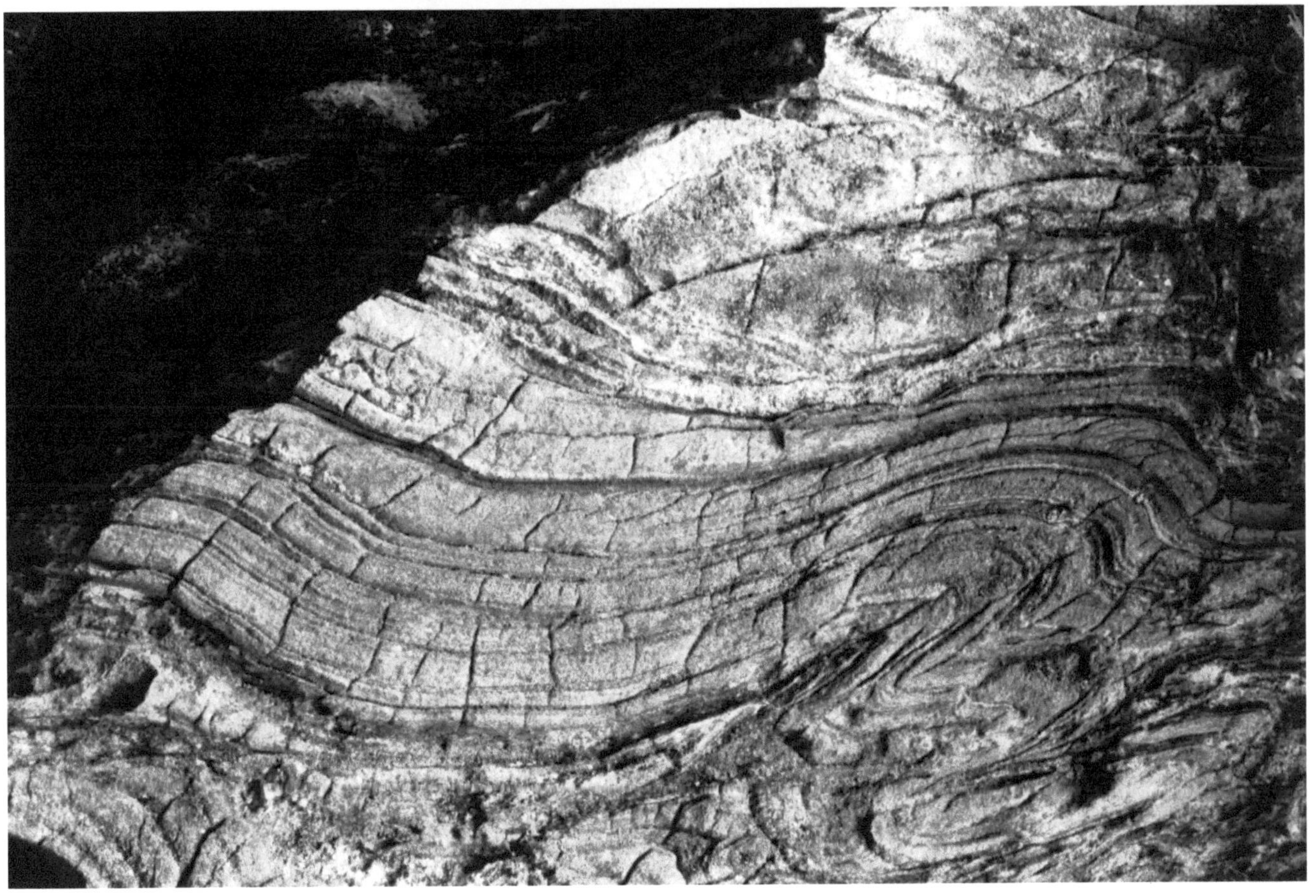

We are stardust, her breath heavy with reverence.

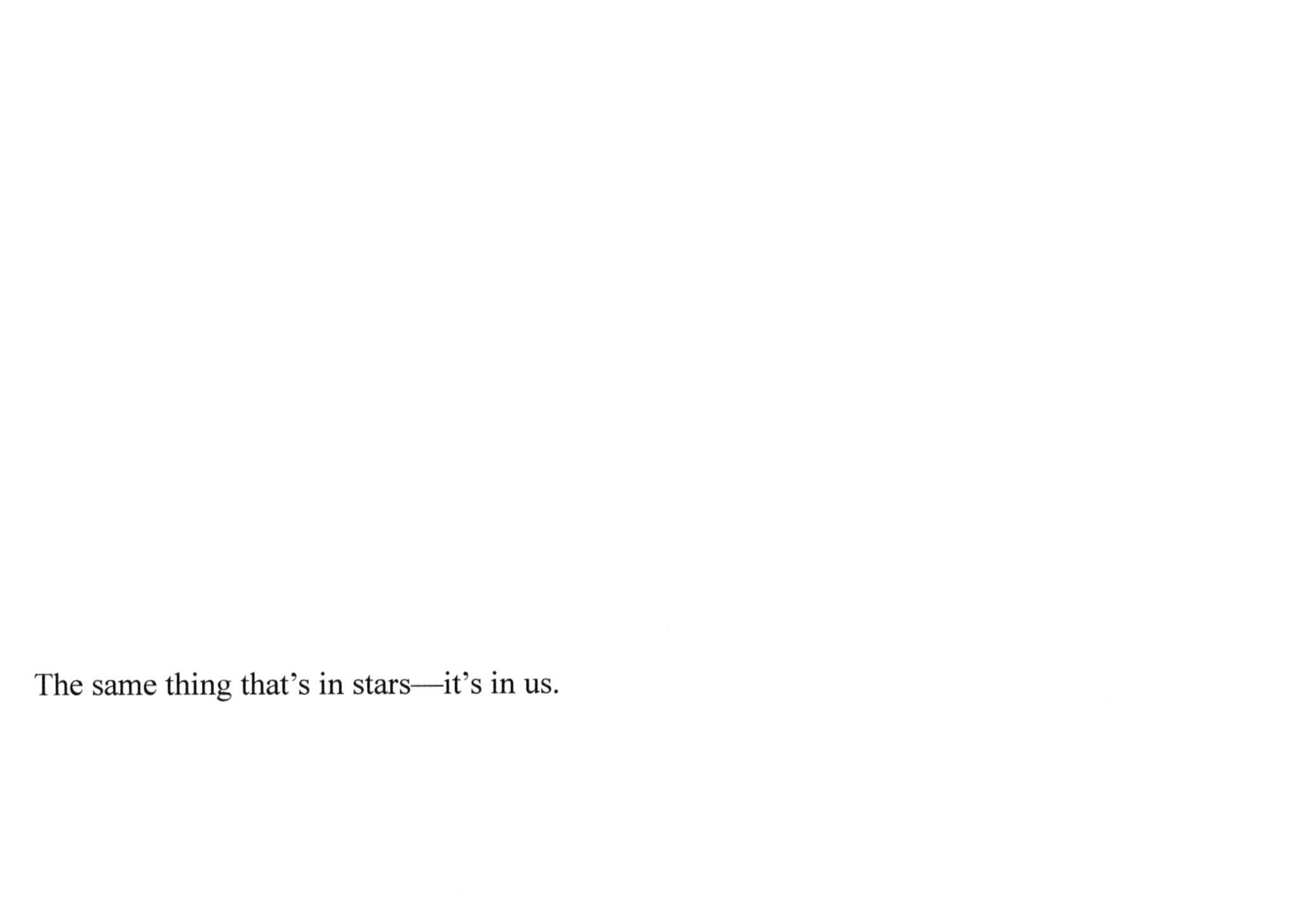

The same thing that's in stars—it's in us.

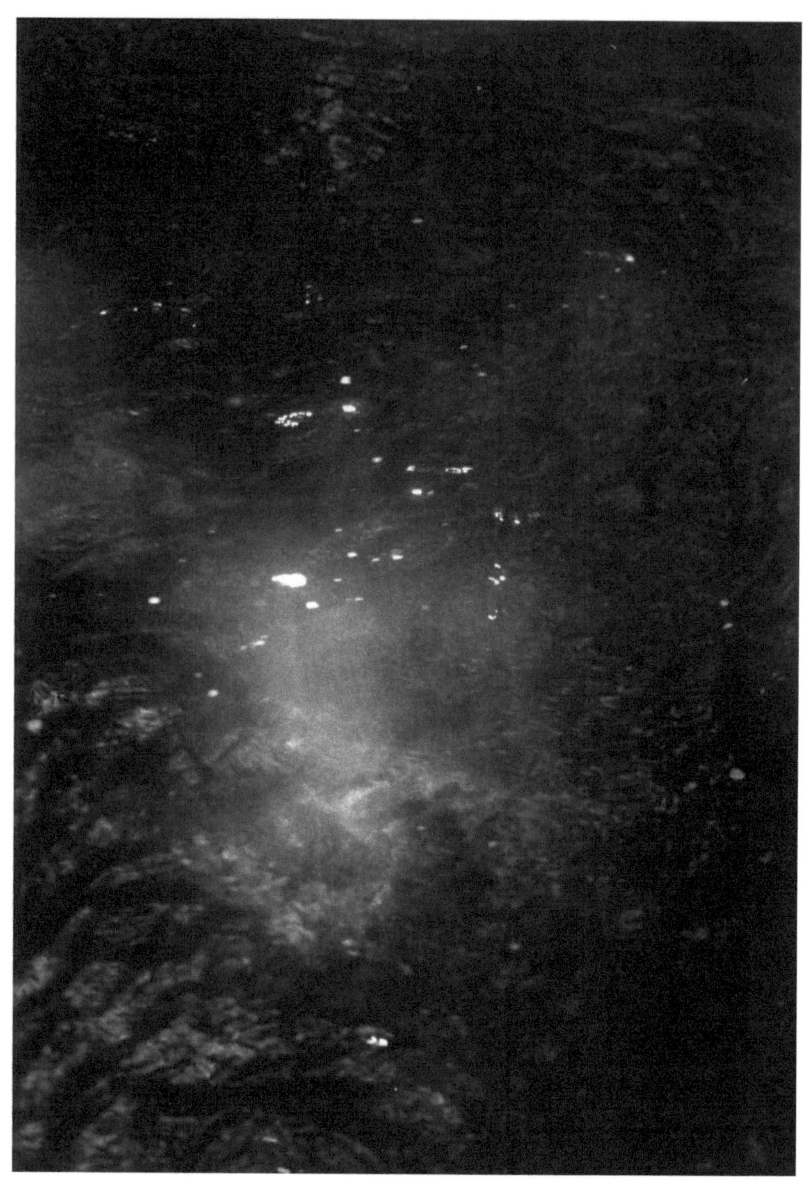

I cannot remember the collapse –

the cooling white, time before time:

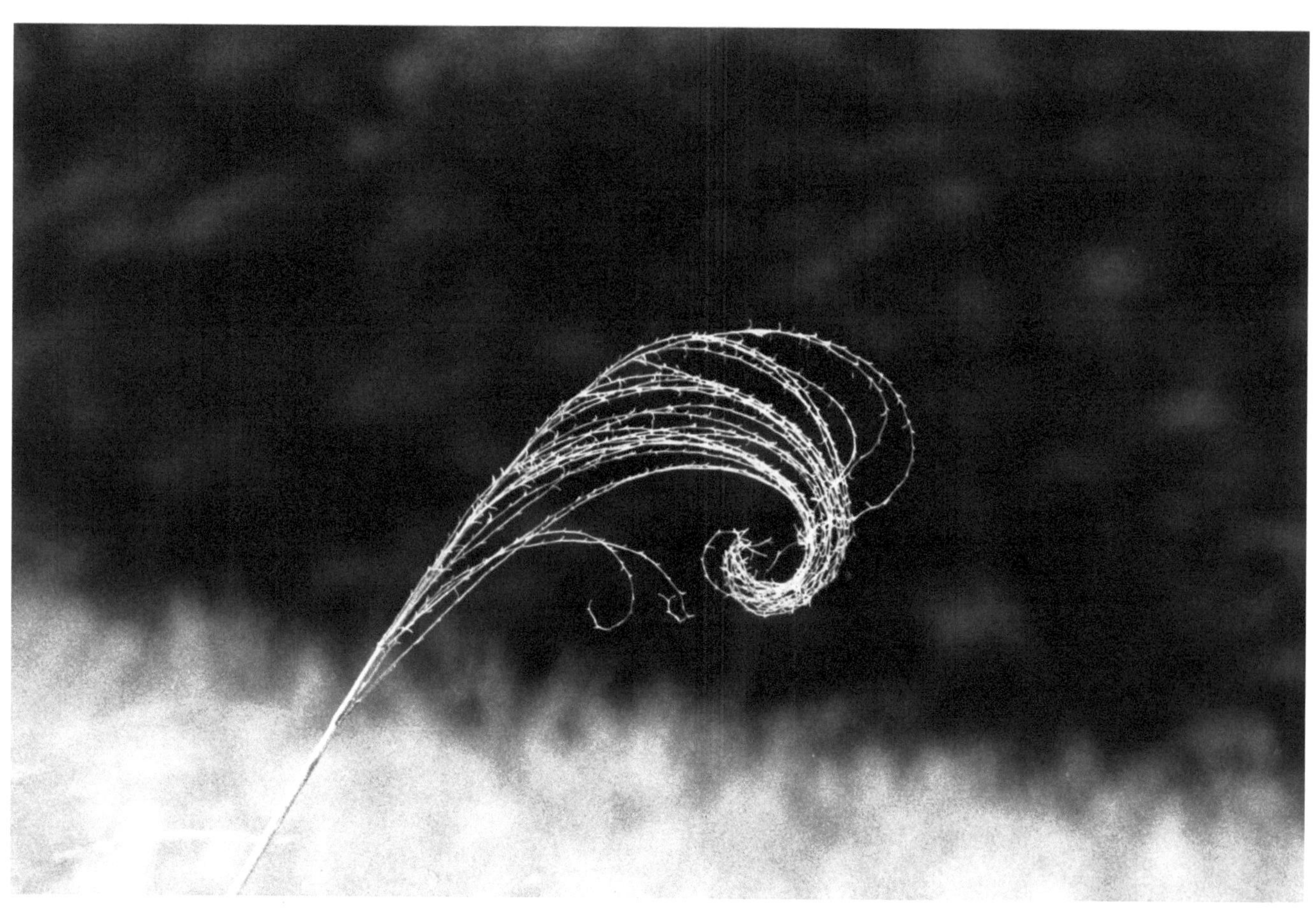

Resplendent, like gossamer hair,

lightly plastered with the milk-sweet sweat of baby labor.

But mothering is remembering:

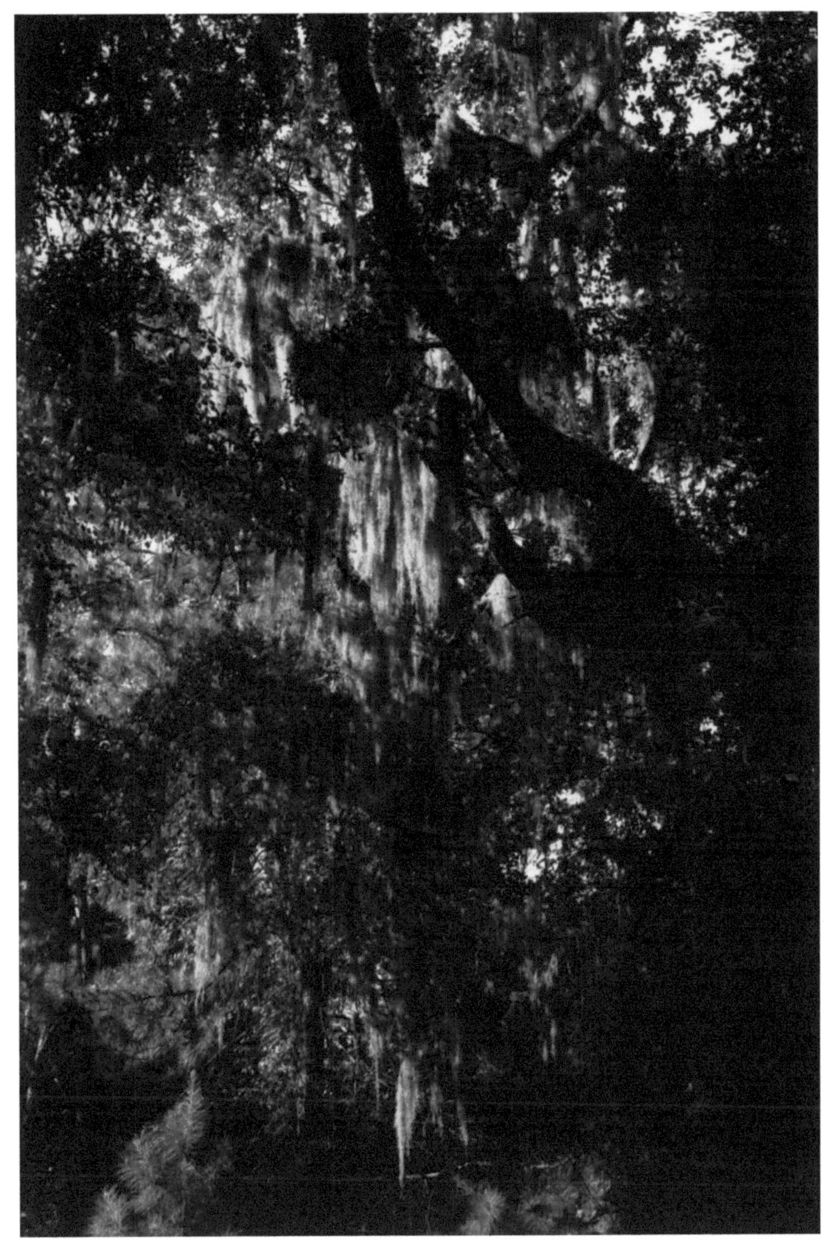

I'm still here.

Still here.

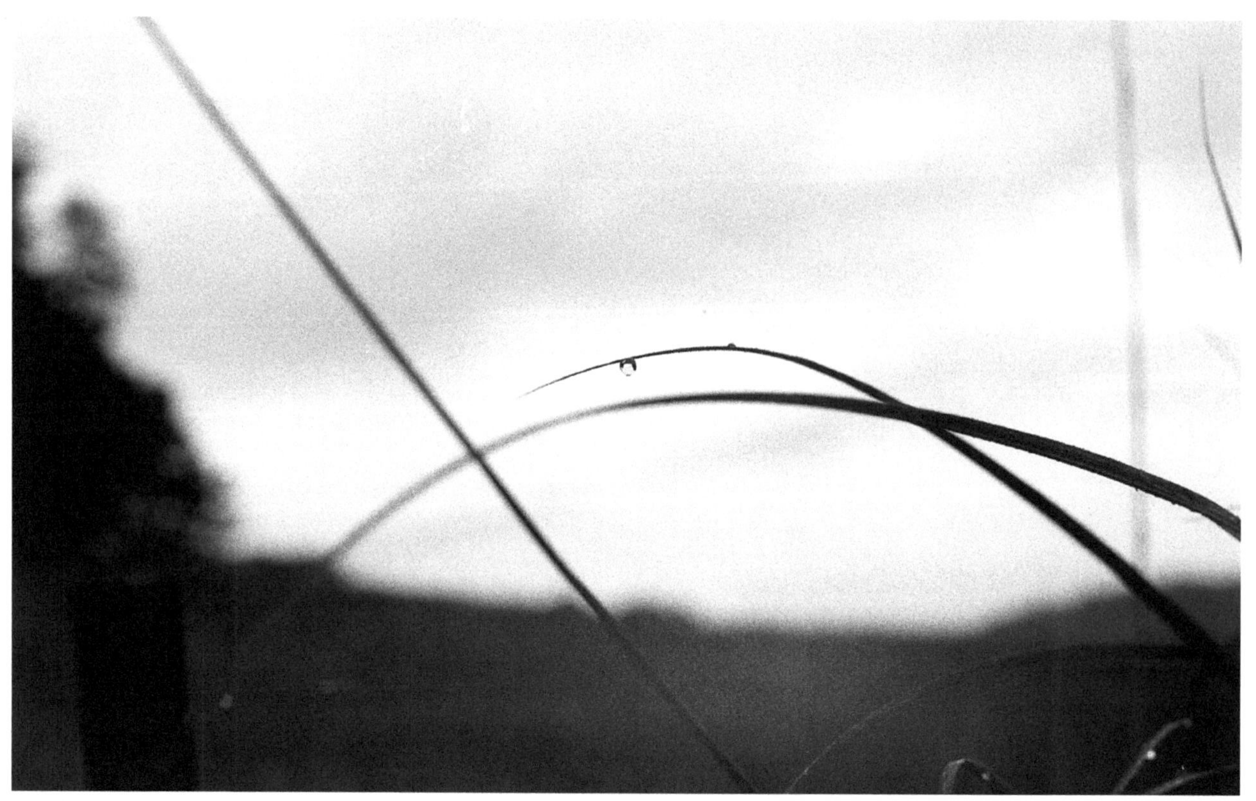

Still here,

her lashes draped long, delicate rose mouth lazily drawing widow's oil.

This is my body: expanding, collapsing, poured out,

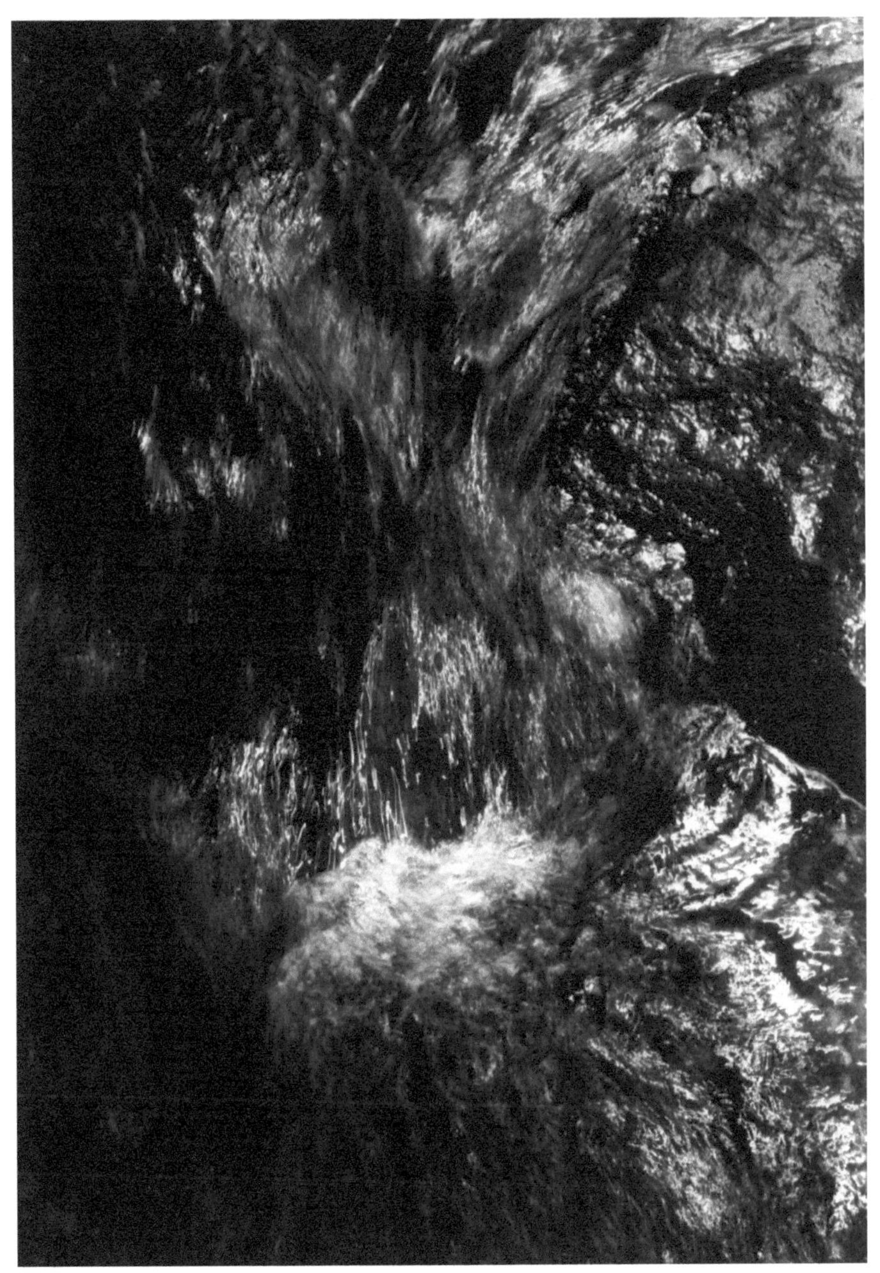

floating

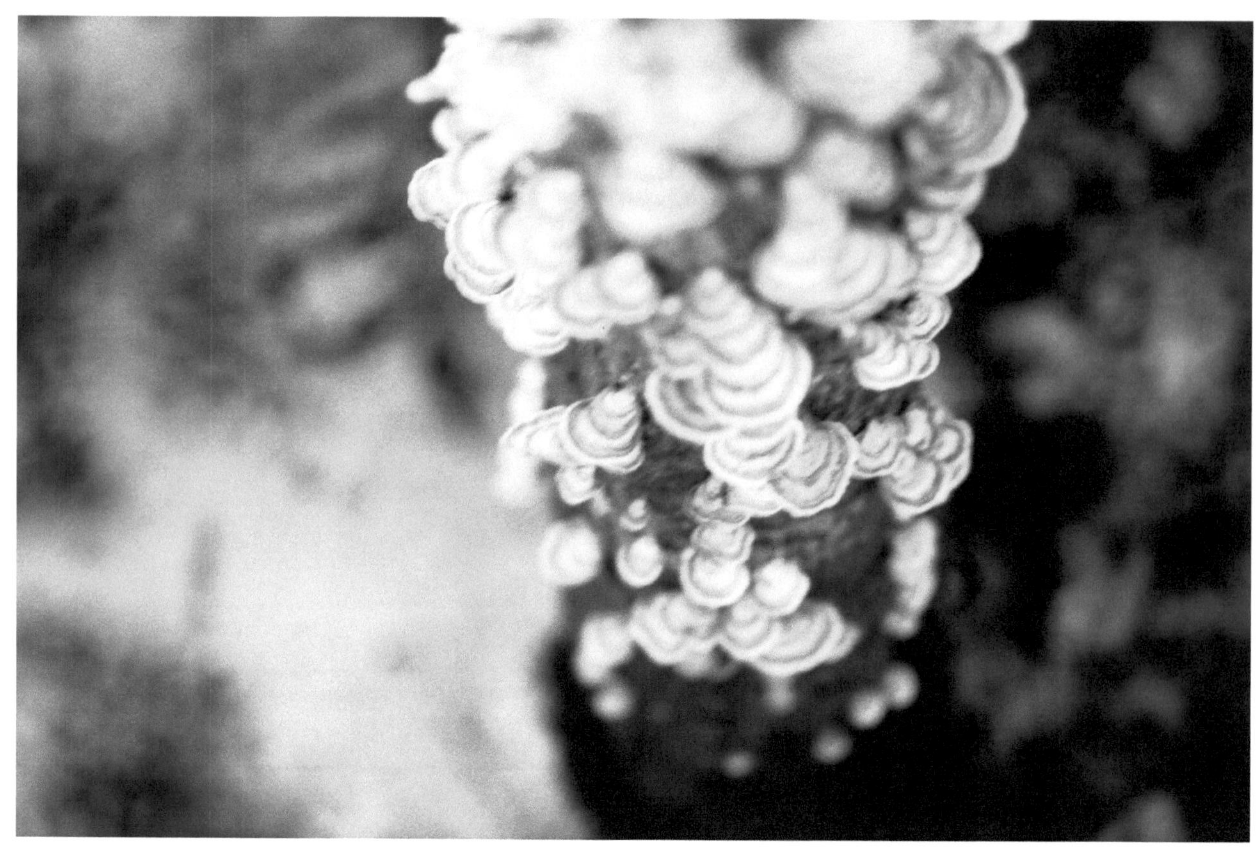

in something like sleep.

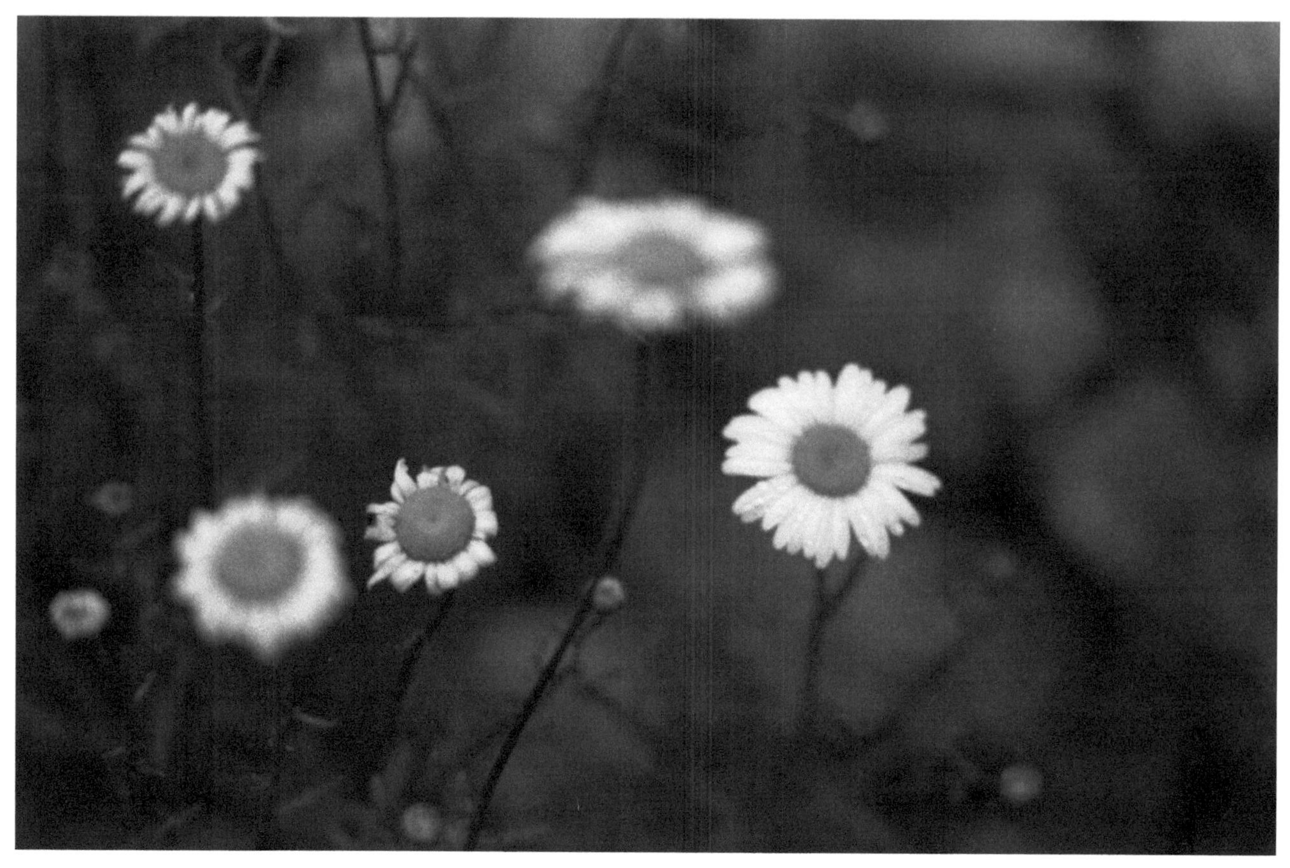

But I figured it out when I woke up.

I figured it out that it was just a dream.

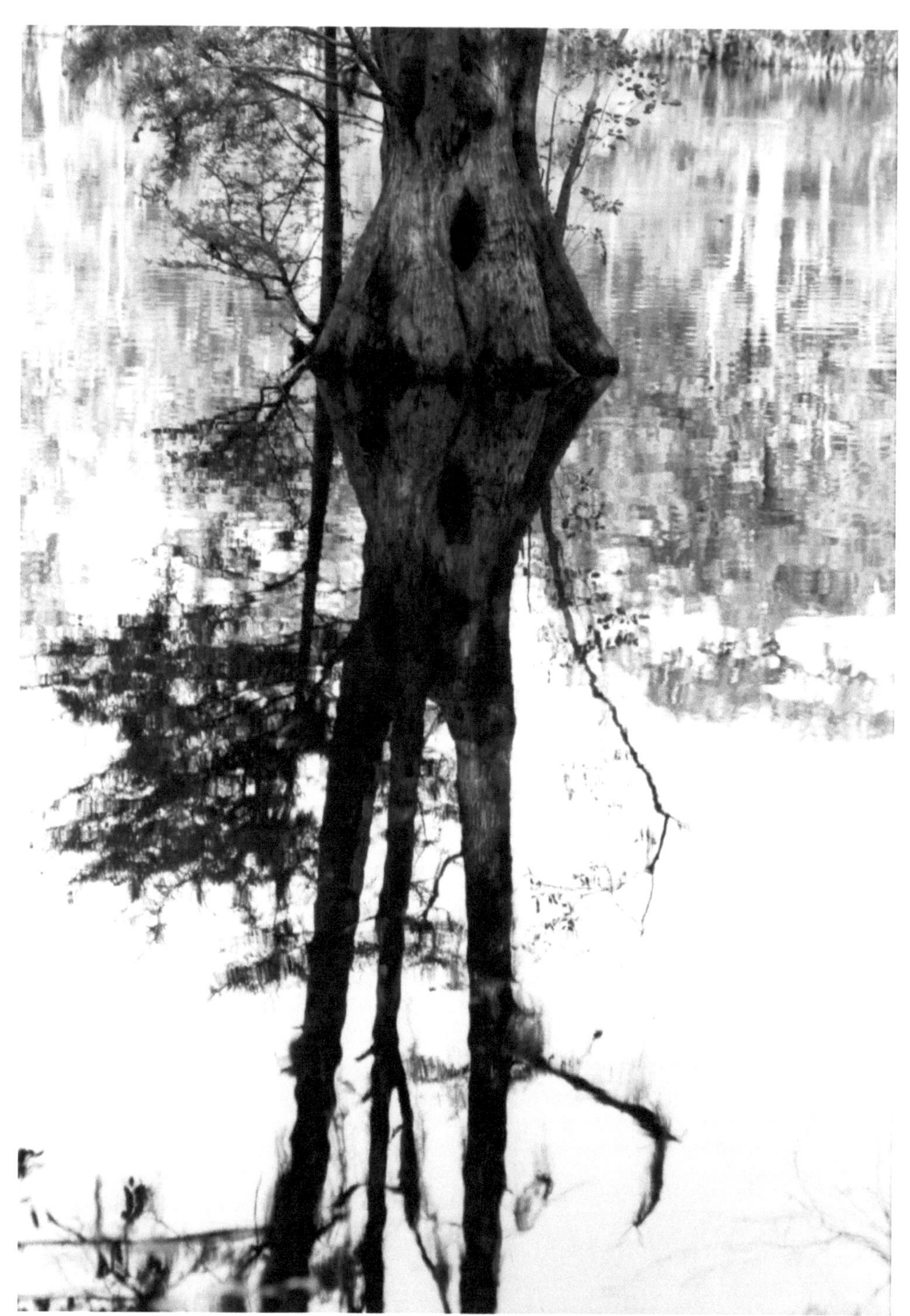

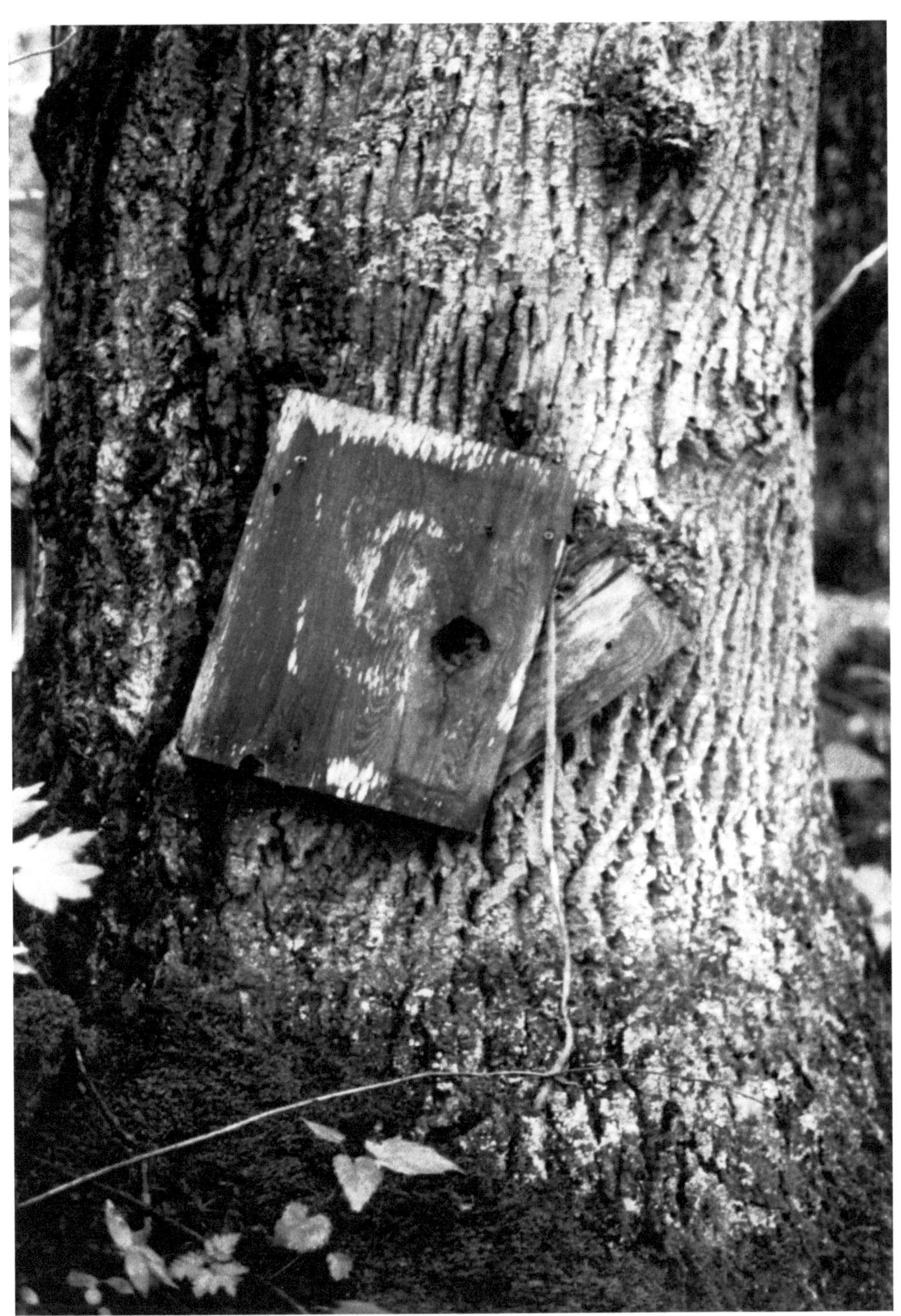

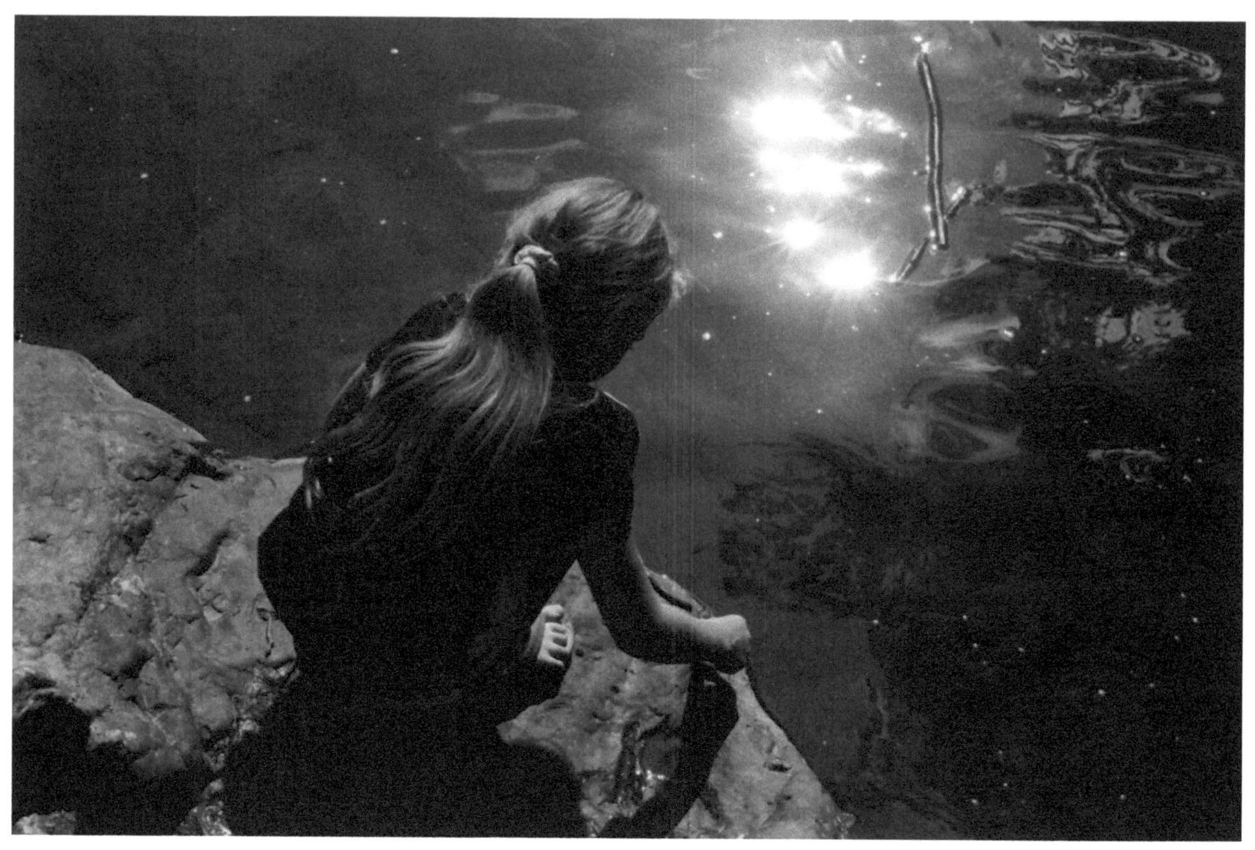

I was the girl in the dream.

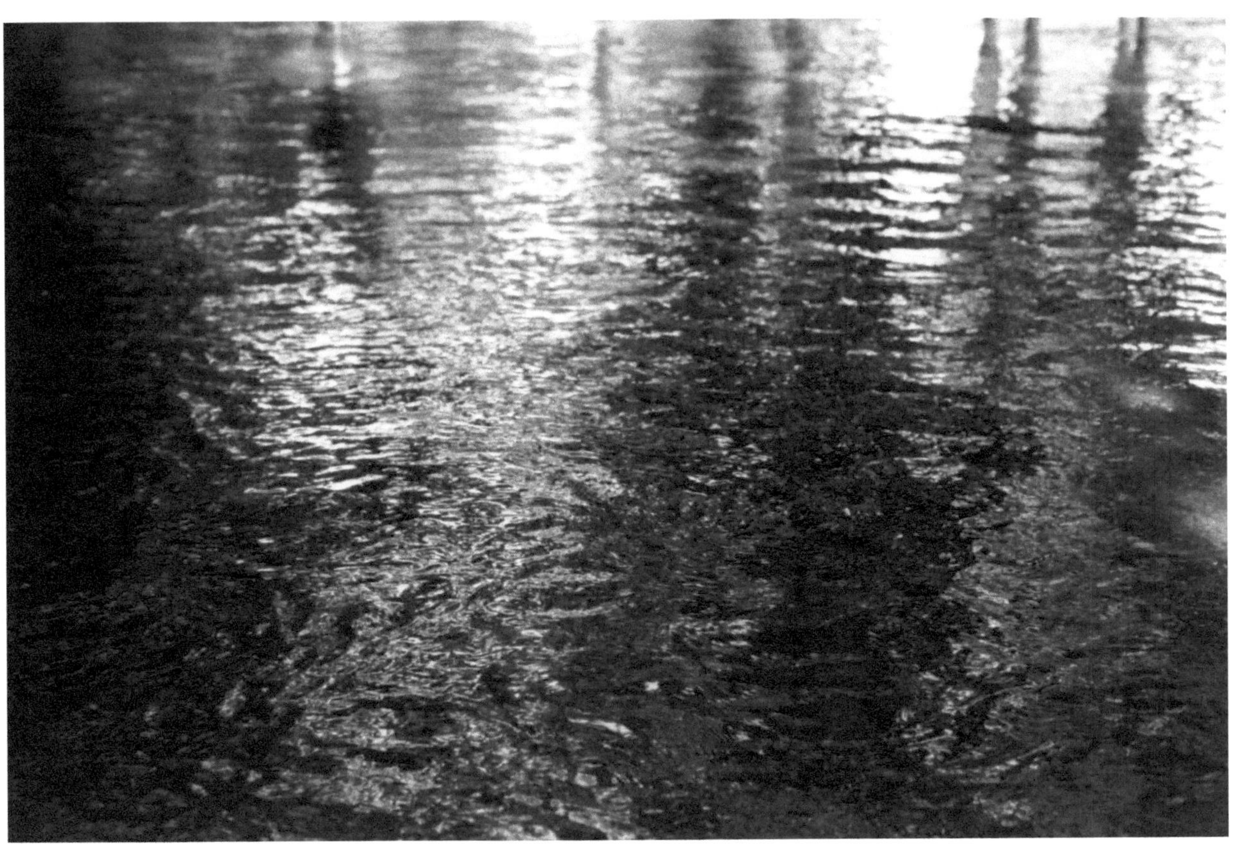

Well, not me exactly.

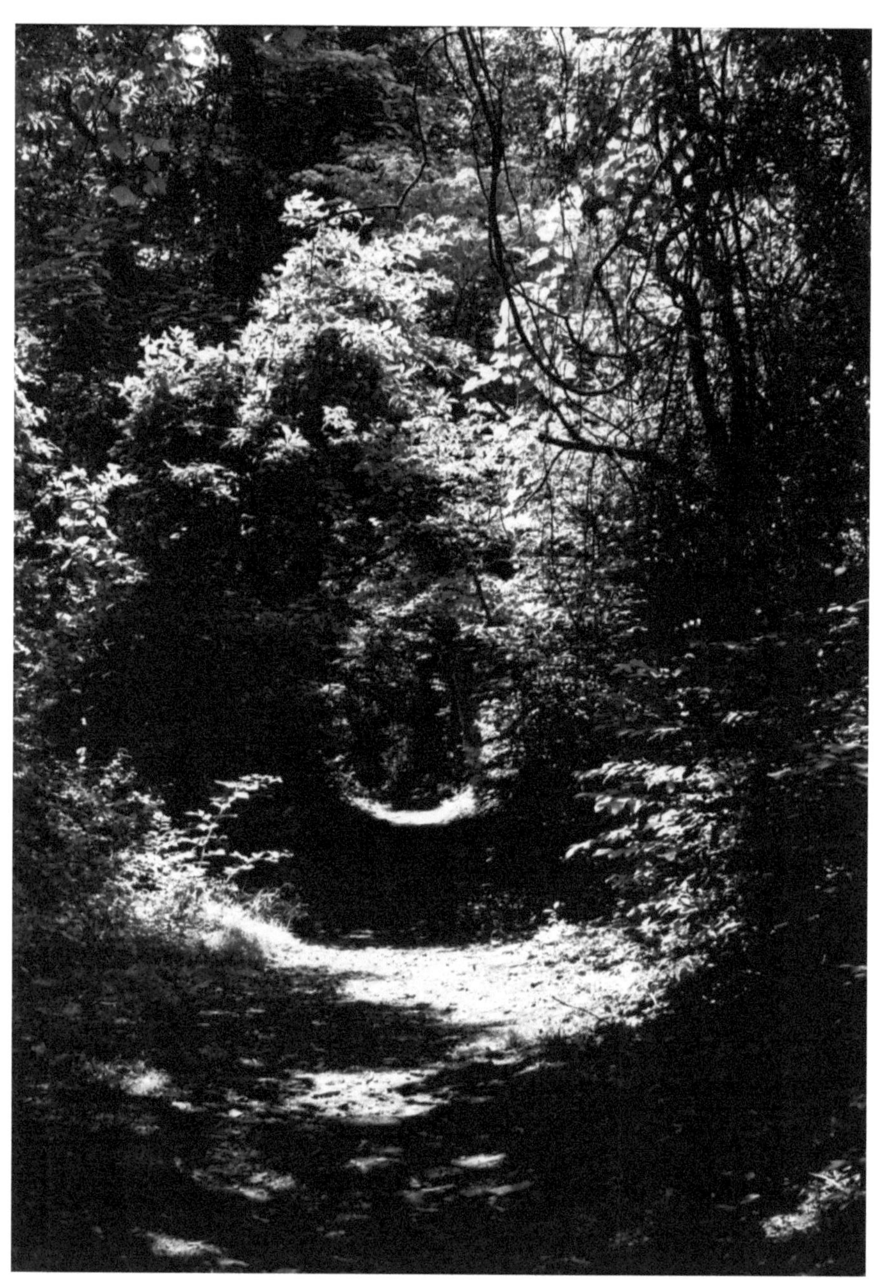

And I remembered

forgotten satisfactions: threading each tine of a fork through a macaroni noodle, plucking

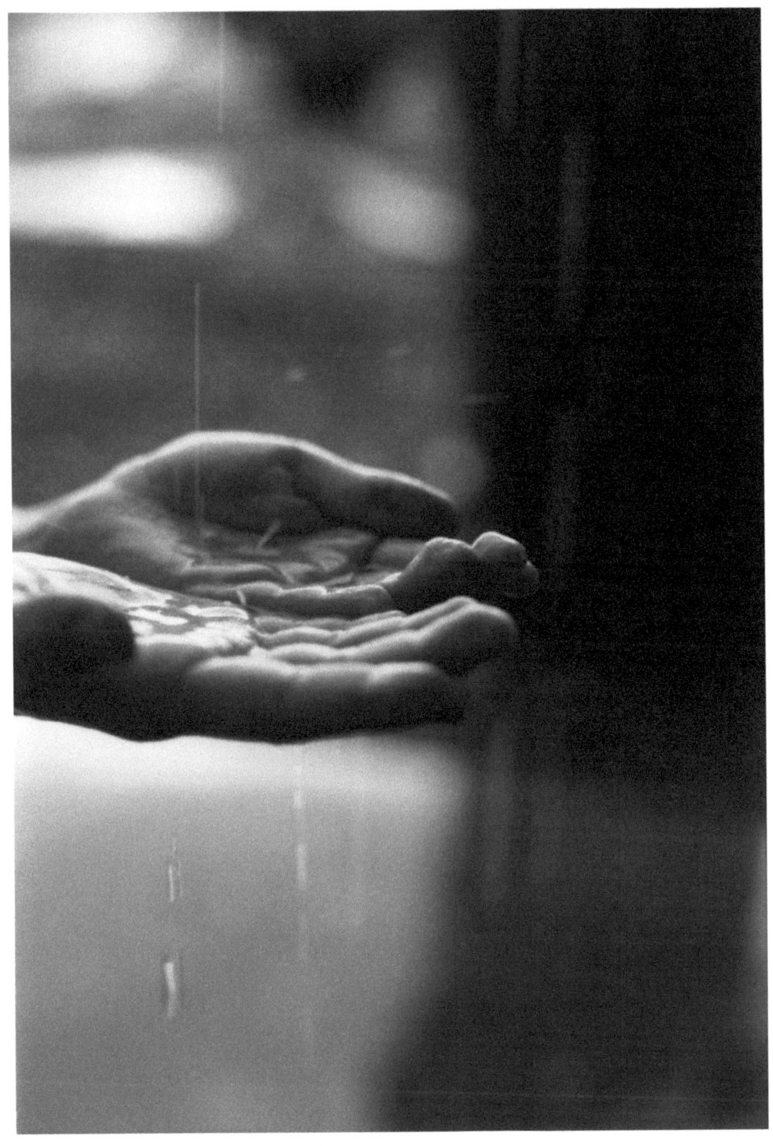

raspberry caps from my fingertips, and how much I love Bach's Magnificat –

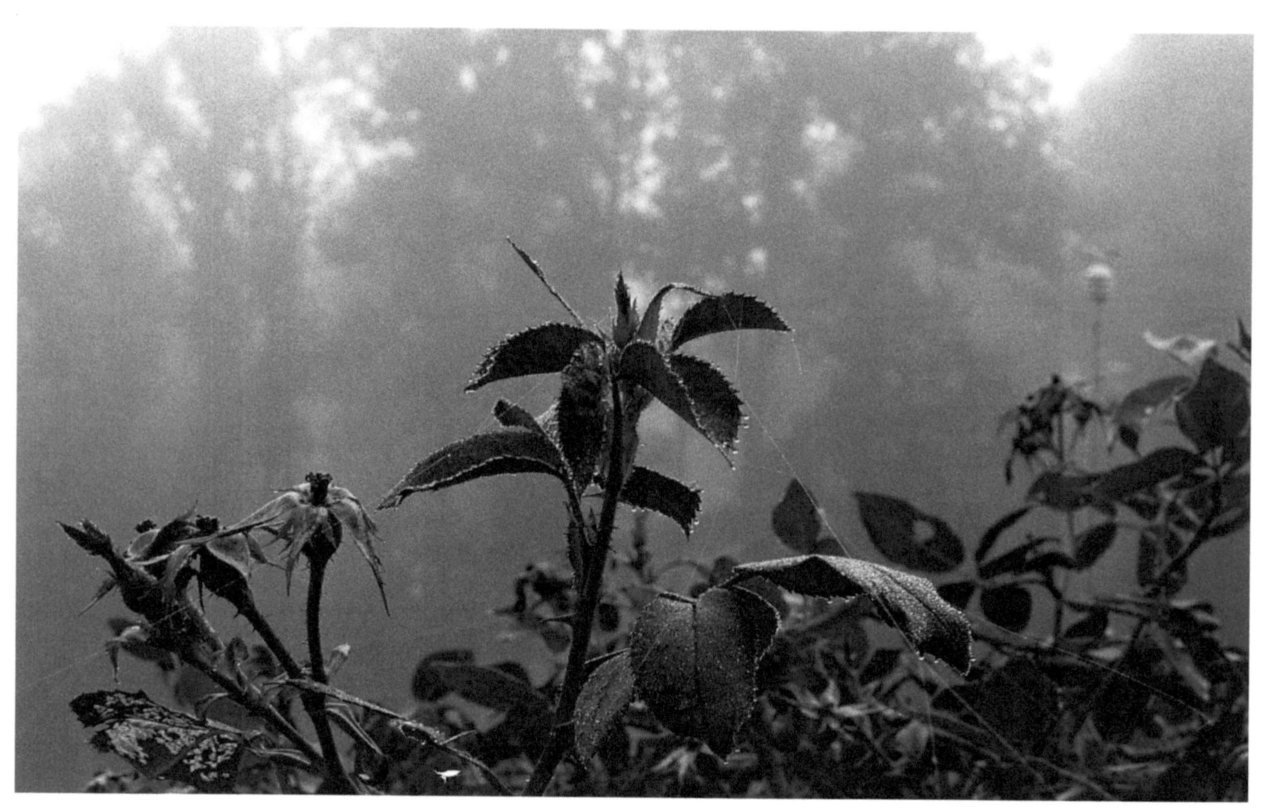

My soul

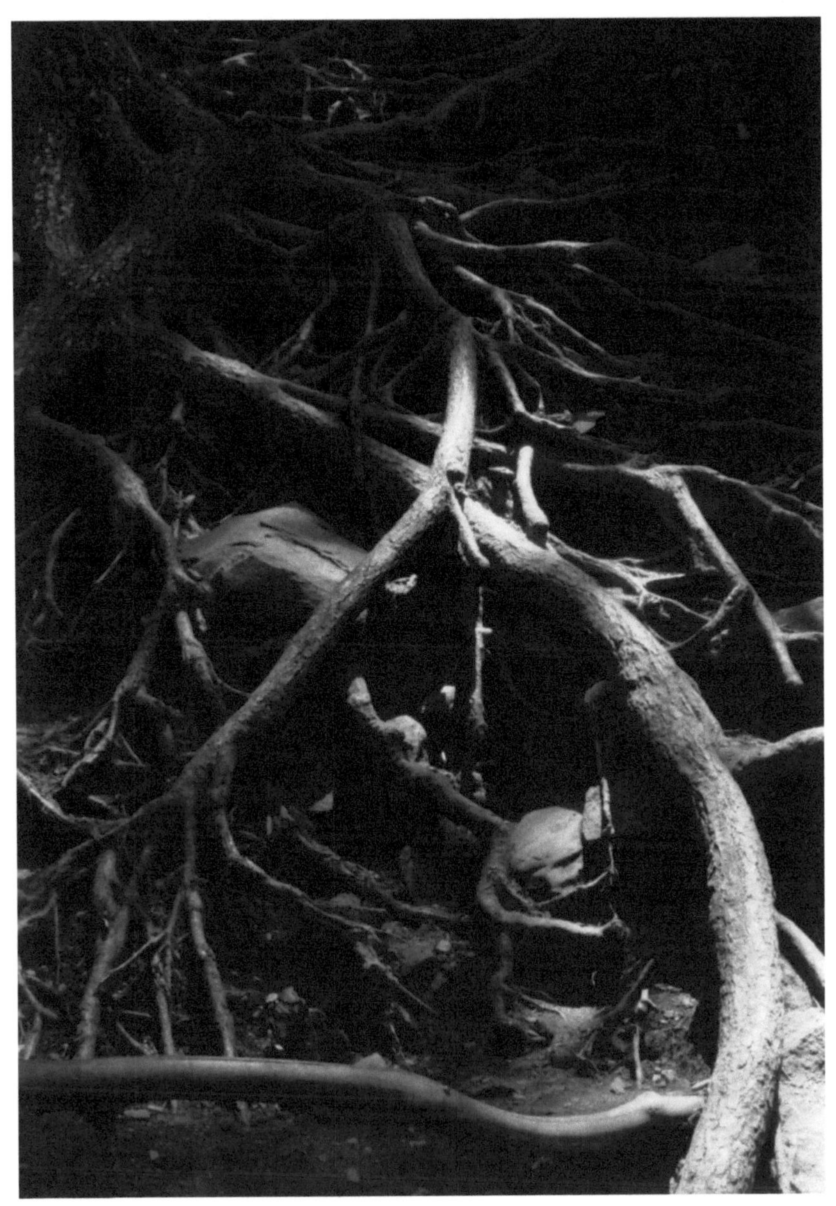

Mommy, I feel like I'm in God's chest.

I've heard God speak to me.

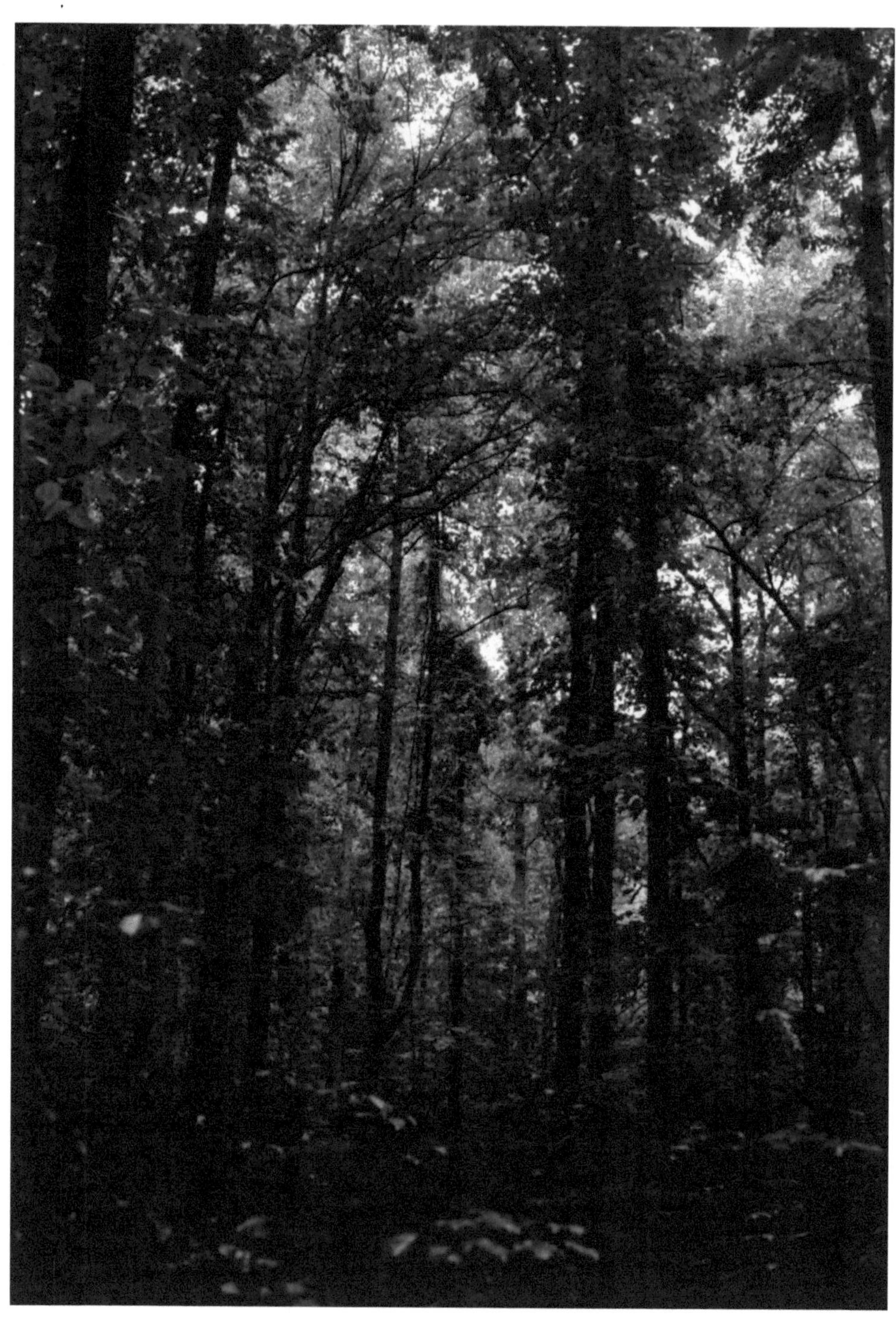

What did God say?

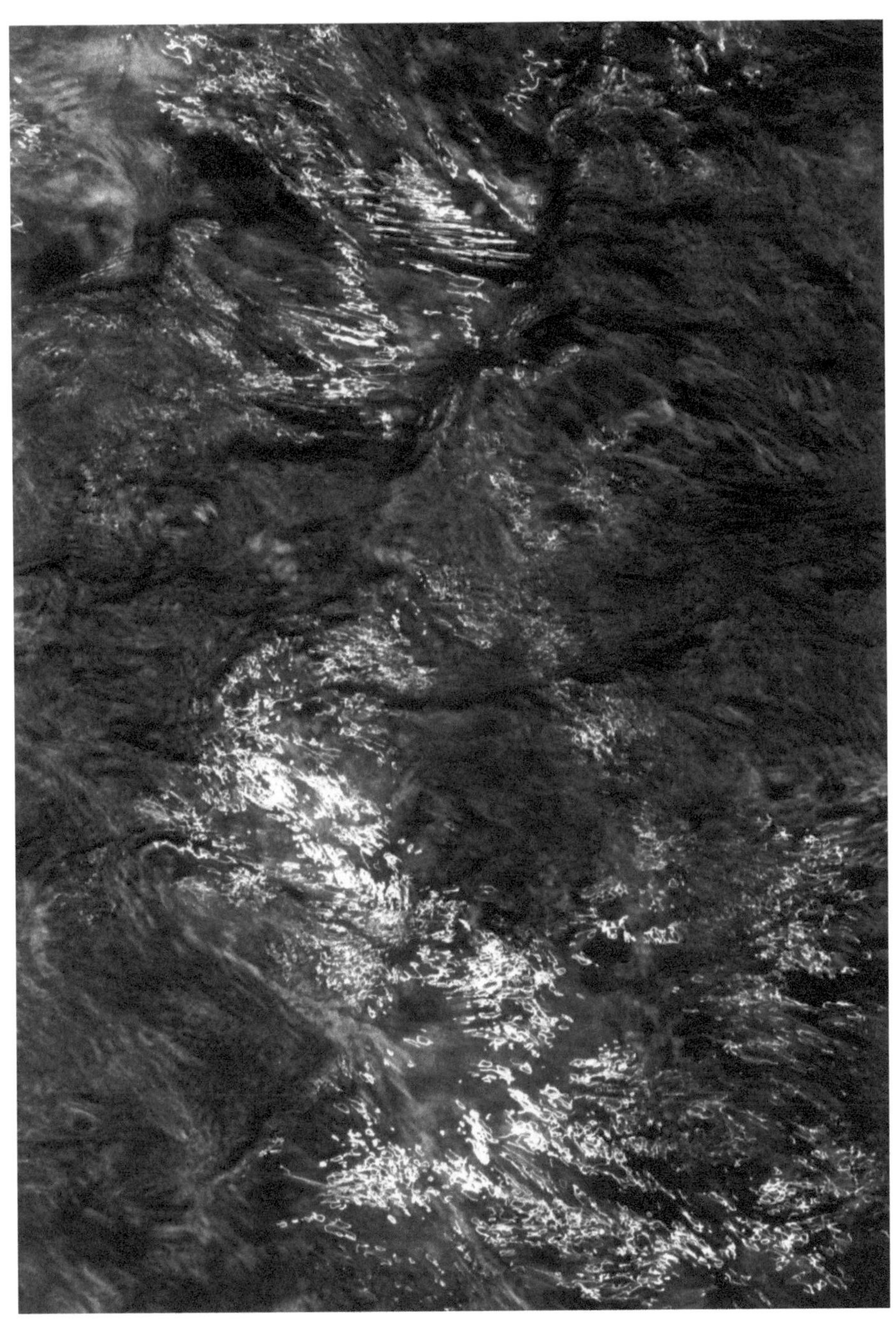

Artists' Statement

So much of parenthood feels as if it's suspended in a gloaming – nights and days blurring into one another, ourselves into our children, them into us. You wonder who said what, and when, and what it meant. Did I tell you that I love you, or was I just asleep?

But dreaming, like play, suspends us in time, and maybe here we touch something common with childhood, the magic of opening categories and questions, bits from you, or me, or somewhere else. And maybe you never find out, maybe no one knows. Maybe it's all a dream. These are pieces of dreams, things said, heard, and perhaps misremembered from a space that's not quite one thing.

How could it ever be?